Panzerf

and other German Infantry Anti-Tank Weapons

Tank-eating made easy! In Manual 77/3 of May 13, 1944, efforts were made to illustrate the principles of antitank combat, in similar style to the "Panther" and "Tiger" manuals, with poems, striking turns of phrase and amusing drawings.

Wolfgang Fleischer

Schiffer Military/Aviation History
Atglen, PA

BIBLIOGRAPHY

- Militärisches Zwischenarchiv, Potsdam WF 02/6721, WF 03/3207, WF 03/32573, WF 03/34695, WF 10/13676, WF 10/21223;
- H.Dv. 220/4b, Mines and Mine Fuzes, Berlin 1944;
- H.Dv. 298/20c, Close Antitank Combat, Berlin 1944
- H.Dv. 469/4, Guidelines for Close Antitank Combat, Berlin 1942;
- Manual 77/3, The Panzerknacker, Berlin 1944;
- D 560/2, 3 and 4, The Panzerfaust, Berlin 1944;
- Waffenblatt No. 7 (Infantry), Feb. 13, 1943;
- Chamberlain/Gander, Anti-Tank Weapons;
- Fleischer, The Development of Antitank Warfare in Germany Between the two World Wars, Potsdam 1986;

PERIODICALS

- Artilleristischer Rundschau
- Berliner Illustrierte Zeitung
- Militärwochenblatt
- Neue Illustrierte Zeitung
- Waffenrevue u.a.m.
- Signal

PHOTO CREDITS

Federal Archives, Koblenz (2), MZA, Potsdam (1), MHM, Dresden (4), Fleischer (15), Hensel (1), ZB, Berlin (2), Thiede (74);

ACKNOWLEDGEMENTS

The author thanks Mr. Wrawczinek (photo research), Mr. Thiese (photography) and Mr. Hensel (drawing) for their assistance.

A drawing from Manual 77/3. Tanks, depending on their design and armament, have a dead angle. In their immediate vicinity the tank crew could see nothing and the weapons, installed in fixed positions, could not be effective. This area must be utilized cleverly through the use of close-combat weapons in antitank combat.

Translated from the German by Dr. Edward Force, Central Connecticut State University.

Printed in the United States of America
ISBN: 0-88740-672-6

This title was originally published under the title, *Deutsche Panzernahbekämpfungsmittel 1917-1945*, by Podzun-Pallas Verlag.

COVER PHOTO

Grenadier with Panzerfaust (large) during firing practice

Translated by Dr. Edward Force, Central Connecticut State University

Published by Schiffer Publishing Ltd.
77 Lower Valley Road
Atglen, PA 19310
Please write for a free catalog.
This book may be purchased from the publisher.
Please include $2.95 postage.
Try your bookstore first.

We are interested in hearing from authors with book ideas on related topics.

IN WORLD WAR I: MEN AGAINST MACHINES

On September 15, 1916, British armored war vehicles (called tanks by the British, Panzer by the Germans) first approached the positions of the German defenders in the Somme area and caused considerable surprise. The use of tanks in World War I provided a new technical means of warfare with a firm position among the fighting forces, despite many unsolved technical and tactical problems. At the same time, though, a new form of combat, that of antitank warfare, was also created.

In World War I the effective weapons to use against tanks were the guns of the artillery. Their task was regarded as providing as effective an artillery battle as possible. This required massive application in hidden firing positions and unified fire control. Only under the impression made by the increasing quantity and quality of tank use by the Entente forces were German field guns put into defensive positions for defense against tanks. They were placed individually and well camouflaged. The champions of massed artillery deployment naturally saw this as a weakening of the weapons' strength. Opposition resulting from this, along with already existing problems with the tanks and their use, hindered the development of effective antitank defense in the German Army. The significance of the tank was played down. As a result, the development of effective new antitank weapons began much too late. They included a 13 mm machine gun for use against tanks and aircraft (TuF-MG), a 13 mm antitank gun and various types of heavy antitank guns.

In the "Tank Battle of Cambrai" in November of 1917, in which, for the first time, several hundred British tanks made a mass attack on the German defensive lines, the failings finally became obvious. Now improvisation was called for. In many places, the close combat of determined individual soldiers against tanks was the essence of antitank warfare. The weapons were just as primitive as the methods, which were born of necessity. "Men against machines," this basic tone characterized the headlines of the reports on the "tank battle"

in the press at that time. But the reports included very little about the critical situations involved and the psychological demands to which the troops were exposed. The use of steel-core ammunition, fired from rifles or machine guns, was not very successful. It was better to aim individual rifle bullets, or pinpoint machine-gun fire, using normal pointed bullets, at the tank's observation slits. The lead bullets broke up on impact and sprayed into the interior of the tank. Lead particles could cause serious injuries to the tank crew, especially in the area of their faces. The effect was only hindering, not destructive. Face masks for the crews and better observation ports soon limited this form of antitank action.

For the infantry it was difficult to attack tanks successfully as long as the tanks were in motion. If artillery shells had destroyed the tracks or the vehicles had become stuck in rough country, ditches or shell craters, then the infantry's chances were better. In many cases, the tank crews were really besieged in their vehicles. If they received no help, their fate was sealed. The possibilities of seeing and observing, like the effective potential of the tanks' weapons, were limited to certain areas. There were dead angles. In addition, sounds from outside the tank could scarcely be evaluated by the crew for the disposition of defensive combat. In the truest sense, they were almost blind and deaf.

The attackers tried to blind the tank crew by throwing single – or if they were not effective enough, clustered – hand grenades under the tank or on top of it. Very brave men even climbed onto the vehicle and tried to make openings, with shovels or side arms, through which they could throw explosive charges. They stuffed observation openings and weapon ports with earth and bunches of grass. And often it happened that only mine launchers or guns, brought to the site, would make an end to hours of combat with a well-aimed shot. In addition, a bounty of 500 Marks was paid for every tank put out of action.

A contemporary portrayal shows a confrontation between infantry and tanks on the battlefield.

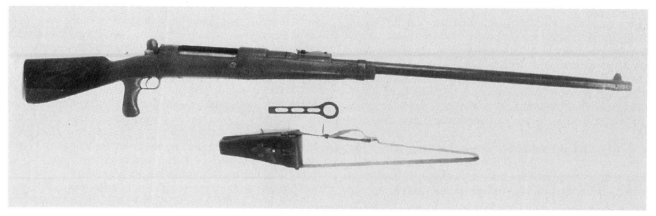

The Tank Rifle 18 with its accessories. It was the first special infantry weapon for use against tanks and inspired various imitations after World War I. The bullet, weighing 52 grams, reached an initial velocity of 770 m/sec. In general, the tank rifle was regarded as too heavy and its recoil too great.

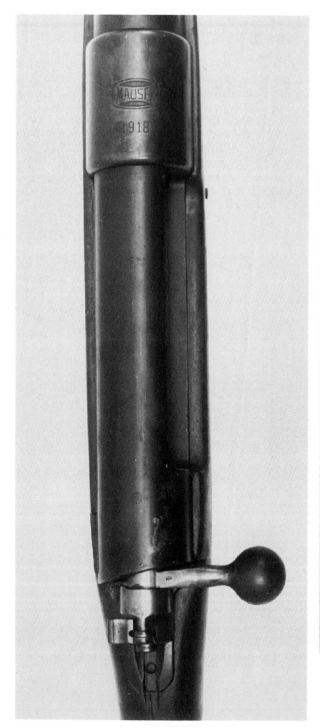

Left:
The breech of the Tank Rifle 18. Note the emblem of the manufacturer, the firm of Mauser, and under it the year of manufacture, 1918. It also bears the lettering "TUF HÜLSE."

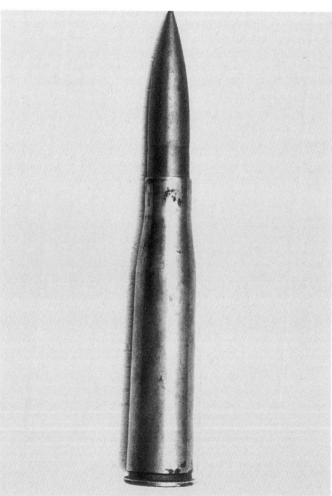

Above:
The 13 mm cartridge is 135 mm long. The weight of a complete cartridge was 117 grams. They were produced by the Polte firm of Magedburg.

The development of a 13 mm machine gun for use against tanks and aircraft (the TuF-MG) could not be brought to conclusion at the desired speed. Only in March of 1918 did its production begin. On December 3, 1917, under the pressure of the heavy fighting around Cambrai, did the Mauser firm begin the development of the tank rifle. The first special anti-tank weapon for the infantry came into being. It was 1680 mm long, weighed 17.3 kilograms, and could penetrate armor plate 25 mm thick. Its effective was sufficient to fight British and French tanks. Available reports from French tank crews, whose vehicles were often penetrated by the steel-core bullets, confirm this. The infantry was no longer unprotected. To be sure, this weapon reached the troops too late and in meager quantities. Thirty thousand tank rifles were ordered. In all, 15,800 were produced, 4632 of which were in the hands of the troops on September 4, 1918. At this time, the fighting forces could already bring several thousand tanks into action.

A practice which should not be undervalued in improving antitank warfare, including that of the infantry, was the issuing of recognition leaflets. They portrayed known types of tanks and showed their vulnerable spots. In 1918 the first drills were held in which combat against captured tanks was portrayed under real conditions. In addition to mines, hand grenades, smoke bombs and other weapons, small flamethrowers (KleiF) were also utilized.

Right: A French soldier with a captured Tank Rifle. On August 11, 1918, two tanks of the 15th Tank Squadron of the French Army were put out of action within a short time, and five men were wounded, when the Germans opened fire with Tank Rifles.

British "Whippet" tanks have broken through the German positions and encountered ready reserves of infantry, among whom panic breaks out. This contemporary portrayal illustrates a situation on the western front in the summer of 1918.

Machine guns – here the light 08/15 machine gun – were not designed for antitank warfare. Armor plate six to eight mm thick could be penetrated. In the Reichswehr they, along with hand grenades and a few T-mines, were the only weapons available to the troops for antitank action by the infantry.

BETWEEN THE WARS – SELF-DEFENSE AGAINST TANKS

After 1918, efforts were made in Germany to evaluate the experiences of the war properly. The mass deployment of tanks by the Entente forces was recognized as one of the reasons for the German defeat in this war. Along with that, deficiencies in antitank combat were admitted. In the Reichswehr, a differentiation was made between active and passive antitank combat. The passive type included utilization of terrain by, for example, locating gun positions in terrain that was impassible for tanks or could be made more so by the work of engineers (with ditches, barricades, traps).

Active antitank defense was characterized by the use of appropriate weapons. Naturally, the emphasis was placed on the guns of the field artillery. In Germany, this included special antitank guns. The military had recognized their value, and their development had proceeded under the strictest secrecy because of the Treaty of Versailles.

But another feature of active antitank warfare was close combat directed against tanks, which still had an atmosphere of improvisation out of necessity about it. Hand grenades, mines and flamethrowers were intended for this purpose. A report on available artillery and infantry weapons in the Reichswehr as of September 5, 1932 is of interest; It includes 1074 13 mm "Tank Rifles" from World War I, which had been banned by the regulations of the Treaty of Versailles. In the Reichswehr's developmental program of 1929 there was also mention of a Panzerbüchse. Its development had to be halted for financial reasons.

An important war experience of general significance was a requirement that the soldiers had to be specifically trained if they were to be used as an effective part of antitank combat.

"Tanks (are) to be spotted and destroyed at their servicing and starting positions." This was above all a task for the artillery, already formulated in the D.V. P1 No. 487, "Conduct and Combat of Fixed Weapons", of 1921. This frontal defense against tanks was correct in principle. Thus critical situations for the infantry were supposed to be ruled out in advance. This position lacked a real basis on account of the variety and numbers of tanks used by the armies. Features in the qualitative development of the tank, including heavier armor, better weapons and greater mobility, constantly offered possibilities of overcoming antitank measures and rolling over infantry forces. It was not by chance that this subject of infantry defense against tanks was constantly to be seen in the technical press. Problems in the maintenance of fighting morale had to be dealt with, a feeling of being "crippled and helpless" against the tank had to be eliminated. It is questionable whether the self-loading rifle for close combat against tanks, suggested in 1925 by Dipl.Ing. W. Brandt, was suitable. Other authors regarded special explosive charges, rifle grenades and Panzerbüchse weapons as purposeful. Makeshift measures were also discussed. For instance, in Morocco from 1921 to 1926, the Riff revolutionaries often brought French tanks to a standstill by pushing iron rods into their running gear. In Spain in 1936-39, dynamite charges and incendiary bombs played a role in antitank warfare.

The significance of successfully involving the infantry in antitank action was undervalued in Germany before World War II, being regarded as not very important for a modern army. Nevertheless, the Wehrmacht possessed around 11,000 3.7 cm antitank guns in 1939. The concept of "close antitank combat" thus became a part of pertinent requirements only during the war itself. In the D 87 "Guidelines for antitank warfare with all weapons" of May 2, 1936, there were still references to "necessary emergency action against tanks."

WORLD WAR II – CLOSE ANTITANK COMBAT

Production of the Panzerbüchse 38 was begun in 1938. It had a complicated breech and was delivered only in small numbers. In Poland there were 62 in service. The simplified Panzerbüchse 39 followed in 1939 and was introduced among the Panzerbüchse troops of the rifle companies. 9645 of these weapons reached the troops in 1940.

Both Panzerbüchse types fired the 7.92 mm SmK H Rs L-Spur cartridge. The bullet, weighing 14.6 grams, could penetrate steel 25 mm thick. With this weapon, the infantry was supposed to be able, in mobile warfare, to have an easier time fighting off the attacks of light armored reconnaissance vehicles that could appear unexpectedly. Its use against tanks was questionable from the start, for at this time the transition to armor that was secure from shells was completed. This cast doubt on the whole question of the continuing development of earlier Panzerbüchse types, which was still going on then, including those with calibers of up to 20 mm. This also sealed the fate of the Waffen-SS designs, which included a 7.92 mm Panzerbüchse, the M SS 41.

The heavy Panzerbüchse 41, which came close to the antitank guns in terms of its size and weight and exceeded them in penetrating power, is also noteworthy. It had a conical barrel from which flanged shells with hard-metal cores were fired.

At first, the most effective close-combat antitank weapon used by the Wehrmacht was the T-mine, which had been introduced among the engineers. The T-mine 29 had already been developed in the days of the Reichswehr. According to a planning study of January 30, 1932, 61,648 of them were to be built, with push or pull triggers. The last of them were disposed of in 1937. In the mid-thirties an improved model, the T-mine 35, was introduced. It was able to penetrate 80 mm of steel armor plate. At first it was produced in limited numbers; in January of 1939, 36,060 were delivered. In view of the increasing importance of the T-mine in the war as a means of barrage as well as in antitank action, it is not surprising that a monthly production of 500,000 was striven for.

The standard weapon of the infantry antitank companies in the rifle regiments and in the antitank units of the divisions was the 3.7 cm Pak L/45 antitank gun. With its antitank shell, it could penetrate 29 mm of steel armor at a distance of 500 meters. This was no longer sufficient in the French campaign of 1940, against British and French tanks with armor 60 to 70 mm thick. In places, crisis situations resulted, which could be remedied by the use of 8.8 cm anti-aircraft guns and field howitzers. This was to change after June 22, 1941. In every sense, the campaign in Russia opened a new dimension, what with the extension of the fronts, the bitterness of the fighting, and the number of weapons involved. The Red Army had more than 18,000 tanks, including 1225 T-34 and 636 KW types with shell-safe armor plate. They lowered the 3.7 cm Pak gun to a mere "tank door-knocking device" and caused complicated combat situations even in the first days of the campaign. Suddenly there was an acute shortage of effective antitank weapons; even the new 5 cm Pak 38 was not sufficient. The few that were available had to be concentrated in the areas especially endangered by tanks. With their great numbers and their ability to operate even in areas that, in terms of terrain, were regarded as safe from tanks, the Russian tanks became an omnipresent opponent of the German infantry. Excellent training and combat experience helped, to be sure, in handling critical situations, but could not be a permanent solution. It was realized that antitank defense was not just the responsibility of a special troop – the Panzerjäger – but rather a complex task to be dealt with by all branches of the army, and in part by the Luftwaffe as well.

The infantry suffered particularly from tank attacks. At times panic resulted, in which the fear of tanks spread. Alarms and commands did not solve the problem; new and effective weapons and combat methods were needed. From then on, the equipping of the infantry with modern close-combat antitank weapons was given more attention. The following general requirements became the basis of them:

A Panzerbüchse troop with the Panzerbüchse 39 during training in the winter of 1940-41. In order to attain an acceptable rate of fire for antitank warfare from the single-shot weapon with its vertical breech, ten or twenty cartridges were carried in special racks attached to the weapon (BA).

Above: A paratroop Panzerbüchse troop with a Panzerbüchse 38. For the paratroops, carrying antitank weapons was an absolute necessity, as their action in Crete showed.

Below: Eastern front, summer 1941. A Panzerbüchse troop and Panzerjäger forces with 5 cm Pak guns on the march.

Above: A mobile Panzerbüchse troop on bicycles. On May 1, 1940, 1469 Panzerbüchse 38 and 39 were on hand. In November of 1939 there had been only 162 of the 38 type.

Below: An infantry spearhead approaches a Russian village in the central sector of the eastern front. The Panzerbüchse troops, off to the left, provide protection.

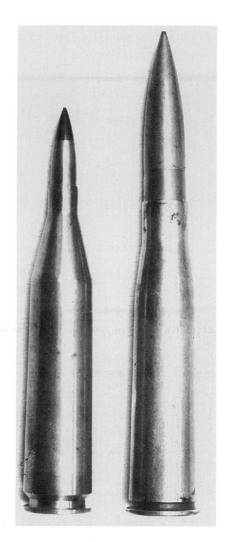

Right: The ammunition for the Panzerbüchse 38 and 39 compared to that of the T-rifle of World War I. The bullet weighed only 14.6 grams, the entire cartridge 84 grams.

A grenade-launcher troop (with 5 cm Grenade Launcher 36) and a Panzerbüchse troop of a rifle company in position.

A Panzerbüchse troop with two Panzerbüchse 39 and complete equipment. The Panzerbüchse weapons are set on the ground.

1. The new close-combat antitank weapons should be able to pen etrate armor thicknesses of 70 to 100 mm reliably without sacrificing their destructive effect in the inside of the vehicle.

2. The customary combat range was to be moved as far as possible forward of the zero-meter mark, so as to achieve an overlapping with the other armor-piercing weapons. T-mines and the new hollow charges were only transitional solutions.

3. Close-combat antitank weapons were to be light and handy, so that the infantry could carry them anywhere.

4. Everyone should be able to be trained to use the new weapons within a very short time. They were to be used in particularly critical combat situations. Therefore smooth handling and easy operation were absolutely necessary.

5. Low production costs should make mass production easier and create an advantageous expenditure-to-use ratio.

It was not easy to achieve all of this. Already existing antitank weapons with heavy bullets had no perspective. That was shown by the Panzerbüchse 39. The heavy Panzerbüchse 41, with a weight of 229 kilograms, was too heavy, as well as much too expensive and complex to produce.

New paths had to be taken. They were suggested by the use of recoilless ammunition, the use of rocket propulsion and the hollow-charge effect. The last had come through its premiere successfully on May 10, 1940, where the hollow charge was used by engineers in the capture of the Belgian forts at Eben Emael.

In the autumn of 1941, numerous efforts to develop new antitank weapons began. By 1943, an almost unimaginable variety of them existed. The Army and Luftwaffe Weapons Offices and the Weapon Academy of the SS in Brünn were working on partly parallel paths.

Only in the course of developmental work did the difficulties appear. Many things were tried, but only a few seemed to be suitable. Only during troop testing did serious deficiencies in operation, functional safety ar effectiveness make themselves known. Only when these faults had been eliminated could large-scale production begin to meet the needs of the troops. Weeks and months pass again and again. Meanwhile the troops at the front had to improvise.

In 1942 and early 1943 the manifold new developments culminated in the large antitank rifle grenade for the cup discharger and the 3 kilogram hollow charge as particularly successful close-combat antitank weapons. In addition, the antitank troops continued to use the T-Mine 35 St. and its successor model, the Sprengbüchse 24 and the 3 kilogram clustered charge. All of these types, as well as the new 3 kilogram hollow charge, were attached directly to the tank to have their effect. If mines could be made to detonate under the tracks of the attacking tank, then only its mobility was limited, but not its firepower. To get close to it, it first had to be blinded. For that purpose, fog hand grenades, rifle grenades, smoke bombs and other special materials were available. If need be, one could throw covers and cloths over the tank. Now the members of the antitank troops had to work according to a precise plan, supporting each other and suiting their actions to the quickly changing situation. Again and again there were tragic accidents. In one case they were able to push a T-mine under the rear end of a T-34, and when it exploded it tore the turret from the hull. It was thrown exactly in the direction where the two soldiers had taken cover, and they were buried under it. Such and similar episodes continued to emphasize the need for more effective close-combat antitank weapons.

The Panzerbüchse M SS 41 resulted from a Waffen SS contract and was based on a Czech development. It was also made to fire the 318 SmK H Rs L-Spur (caliber 7.92 mm) cartridge. Russian armored scout cars and light T-26 tanks could be attacked successfully with it at distances from 20 to 50 meters. Despite well-aimed penetrating shots, it rarely put the tank out of action. This made the further development of the 38, 39 and M SS 41 Panzerbüchse questionable.

With the appearance of the T-34 on the eastern front, the Wehrmacht's antitank defense became a crisis. The infantry's trust in its own antitank capability was shattered. The tendency to panic at the approach of tanks, as stated in a report of the 88th ID of March 1942, could not be eliminated solely by means of education. The quicker introduction of sufficiently effective antitank weapons was urged.

Russian tanks had suffered great losses in 1941-42. In spite of that, they came into being very quickly. The Russian tank industry, located beyond the Ural Mountains, delivered 24,655 tanks in 1942, including 12,553 of the T-34. Additional tanks came from Britain, Canada and the USA via Lend-Lease. After the Allied landings in Italy and northwestern France, the situation became even more complex for Germany. The question of successful antitank defense was no longer just one vital problem – it became a decisive factor in the success or failure of future military operations.

A vital qualitative improvement in the antitank weapons of the infantry was attained with the Panzerfaust and the antitank rocket (Ofenrohr/Panzerschreck). After initial difficulties, success was achieved during 1943 in developing these weapons sufficiently for series production. The 8.8 cm antitank rocket became the essential antitank weapon of numerous infantry Panzerjäger companies, tank-destroyer battalions and the tank-hunting brigades that were established toward the end of the war. They were divided into tank-destroyer squads, which were compelled by the short range of these weapons – less than 200 meters – to take up positions where they could mutually support each other. The Panzerfaust attained even greater significance in close-range antitank action. By constant further development, the originally insignificant range could be increased by 150 meters to a maximum of 300 meters for the Panzerfaust. This weapon combined great penetrating power (200 mm), light weight (5.1 kg), simple handling and low production cost.

With these two weapons, the antitank rocket and the Panzerfaust, it was possible to extend the usual distance for the use of antitank weapons (other than the rifle grenades) farther to the front. In the ideal situation, depth and overlapping of antitank and artillery weapons became possible.

In April of 1944, 2878 enemy tanks were destroyed on the eastern front, 172 of them in close combat. Of these, the lion's share, namely 110, fell to the Panzerfaust, 26 to the rocket. Only nineteen were destroyed by hollow charges and eleven with T-mines. In combat in mountainous and wooded terrain and in large cities, the percentage of tanks destroyed by close-combat weapons was naturally greater.

The Panzerfaust in particular typified the modern, recoilless one-man weapon for antitank combat. It allowed the infantry to fight against tanks at an acceptable distance and with good prospects of success. With the Panzerfaust and the antitank rocket, Germany took a leading position in the realm of close-range antitank combat in the war. Both weapons had great potential for further development, which allowed for heightened performance to match the progress being made in tank construction. The Panzerfaust in particular was cheap to produce, and its use did not depend on any special training. These factors were of remarkably great importance to Germany in the last months of the war. The further development of this type of weapon by the Allies after World War II speaks for the potential of their basic concept.

Parallel to the development and introduction of new antitank weapons, the means and methods of close-range antitank combat training had to be improved on the basis of experience gained at the front. It took up an ever-greater part of the meager time spent on training the troops in the replacement units. Special training courses were supposed to expand on existing knowledge. The directions, tank recognition materials, equipment manuals and training films must be described as truly exemplary.

The heavy Panzerbüchse 41 at Akja, along with the 5 cm Pak 38 L/60 gun.

Tank recognition charts portrayed the armored vehicles of the enemy, showing their typical identifying marks. The surfaces of the tanks that were particularly sensitive to shots were marked.

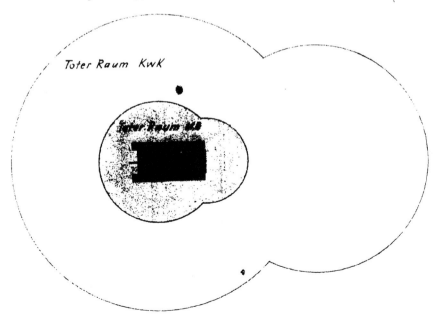

Toter Raum KwK

Toter Raum M.G.

Left:
The dead area of a tank's weapons afforded a sufficient field of activity for close antitank combat.

Above:
For realistic training in close antitank combat, captured tanks, test models (here a new-type Panzerkampfwagen II), or . . .

Right:
Dummies made of wood and linen, on car, truck or ammunition carrier chassis, were used.

Below:
Basic training at Leipzig-Borna in the summer of 1944. An old Assault Gun III is used to train soldiers to let a tank roll over them.

MAKESHIFT CLOSE-COMBAT ANTITANK WEAPONS

In general, close-combat antitank weapons were divided, according to their use, into:

a. Sight-obscuring agents.
b. Destroying agents (explosives and incendiaries, tools).

In the H.Dv. 469/4 "Antitank Defense, All Weapons", of October 7, 1942, it was indicated that, if close-combat weapons should not be available for use, they had to be prepared in a makeshift manner. This included such explosive and barrage materials that were originally intended for a different use but were suitable for antitank combat.

Stick and egg hand grenades could be effective against opened ports and destroyed cooling flaps. To fight against light tanks, the use of stick grenades as clustered charges was possible. For this, the shells of seven stick hand grenades were bound firmly together with wire or cord, and a percussion cap was placed on the central grenade, which was equipped with a stick.

Smoke grenades could be used effectively to blind tank crews. It took a great deal of ability to throw two smoke grenades tied together with string in such a way that they wrapped around the barrel of a tank gun and burned out there, so that the resulting smoke would obscure the tank crew's vision, which was a requirement for the use of other means of close combat. Smoke bombs, flare ammunition and incendiaries could also be used to obscure vision, and if they were not available, earth, paint, cloths, coats and tent canvas could be used. Special blinding equipment was introduced later. Smoke hand grenades were also used along with 20-liter gasoline canisters, which were thrown at the tank, emptied, and ignited by the explosion of the hand grenade.

Following a Russian practice, incendiary bottles were used to set tanks afire. Bottles of any size were filled 2/3 with gasoline and 1/3 with oil or burning oil. Two matches were taped to the bottle and enclosed in wads of tow. Gun wicks were also usable. The various models of T-mines had a wide variety of uses. They were regarded as particularly effective and safe means of destroying tanks. Their explosion could break through 80 to 100 mm of armor plate.

According to how they were used, T-mines were equipped with the T-mine igniter (which worked by pressure), with the Sprengkapselzünder 28 or the pull igniter. According to the combat situation, the explosive charge could thus be utilized to destroy the tank (by damaging the armor plate) or to immobilize it. It took some practice and even more courage for one man to throw the mine under the tank's tracks at the right moment, or to ignite the well-camouflage mine on the tank's path by hand by means of a trigger wire. Movable mine barrages and gliding mines were other types. In the movable mine barrage, called a ramp barricade, four to six T-mines were fastened to a plank and pulled in front of the tank.

When T-mines were not usable, 3-kilogram clustered charges, or the Sprengbüchse 24, could be substituted. Several of these charges could be combined as extended or clustered charges. The Sprengbüchse was useful in destroying weapons, weapon shields and tank-gun barrels. To do this, they were fastened to them, or pushed into the muzzles of large-caliber tank guns. In May of 1942 a manual was issued. In it, the preparation of makeshift 4-kilogram hollow charges using four of the Sprengbüchse and the Sprengkapselzünder 28 igniter was described.

Tools (hatchets, crowbars, shovels and axes) could be used to open or destroy hatches and cooling flaps. Stones and other objects could be shoved into the gun barrels to cause them to explode when fired.

With these types of close antitank combat, two problems were brought together. The individual fighter had to approach the tank as fast as possible and come within touching distance of it, utilizing the tank's weak points. When the charge was ignited, the built-in delay had to be utilized to take cover as far away as possible. It was a laborious and costly fight.

A paratrooper with a steel T-Mine 35.

Left: Makeshift incendiary bottles fitted with matches. In 1940 the Army Weapons Office had already carried out tests of incendiary bottles on captured French tanks. The results were not satisfactory, for the incendiary fluid did not reach the interior.

Below: The Stick Hand Grenade 24 and (at right) the Fog Hand Grenade. Seven or thirteen of the Stick Hand Grenade 24 were used a clustered charges. Fog grenades were used primarily to obscure the tank crew's vision.

Below: Two grenadiers prepare a clustered charge, using seven of the Stick Hand Grenade 24. The percussion cap and fuse are attached to the middle one, which is equipped with a stick.

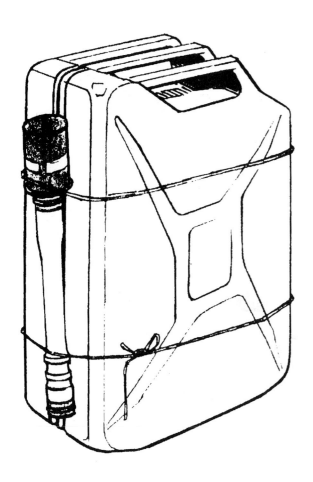

Left and above:
Another makeshift weapon, a 20-liter gasoline canister with a Fog Hand Grenade 39. The Incendiary Igniter 39 for the fog grenade had a delayed action of 4.5 seconds – little time for the close-combat antitank man to take cover.

Above and right:
Two fog cartridges or fog grenades, tied together with a cord or wire about two meters long, could be thrown over the barrel of a tank gun from a short distance and obscure the tank crew's view when they burned.

Two of the T-Mine 42 – with their pressure caps turned toward each other – could be transported in one carrying case. A T-Mine 42 weighed 9.4 kilograms. It could be equipped with an explosive igniter that had a delay of ten seconds.

Below: It took a lot of strength and some practice to throw the heavy mine onto the rear of the tank.

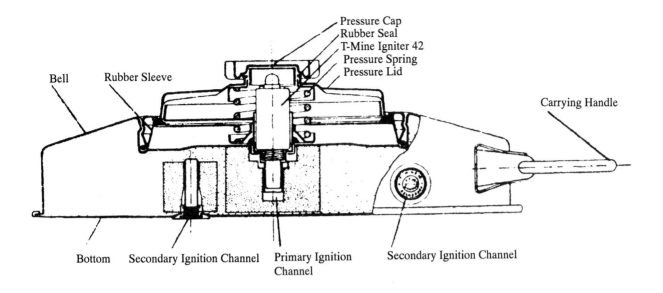

Bell — Rubber Sleeve — Pressure Cap — Rubber Seal — T-Mine Igniter 42 — Pressure Spring — Pressure Lid — Carrying Handle

Bottom — Secondary Ignition Channel — Primary Ignition Channel — Secondary Ignition Channel

Above:
The T-Mine 42 was made according to the same principles as the T-Mine 35; but its movable, ribbed pressure lid took up only one quarter of its upper surface.

Right:
The use of close-combat antitank weapons required thorough preparation. It was promising to await the attacking tanks at bridges, ditches, or in wooded or built-up areas. The cooperation of the antitank fighters was also important.

Below: Various antitank mines, from left to right: T-Mine 35, T-Mine 42, wooden T-Mine.

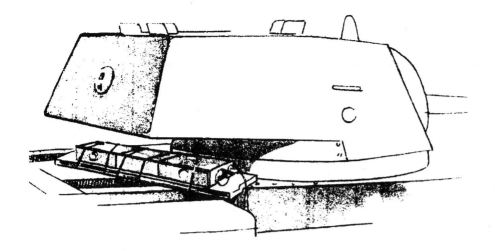

When all close-combat antitank weapons were used up, the 3-kilogram charges used by the engineer platoons could still be utilized. Three of them were combined in clustered or in-line charges and equipped with a percussion cap or 7.5 second fuse. Such a charge, exploded under the rear overhang of the turret, resulted in the destruction of the tank.

ANTITANK WEAPONS FOR FLARE PISTOLS/RIFLE GRENADES

Explosive ammunition could also be fired from rifled or smooth-bore flare pistols (combat pistols). It was simple enough to develop armor-piercing ammunition for these weapons as well, and it offered the possibility of being able to fight against tanks successfully at greater distances. For the smooth-bore flare pistol there was the Wurfpatrone 326 HL/LP cartridge with four control surfaces (which could penetrate 50 mm) as well as the Wurfmine H 62 LP with ring-shaped control surfaces. The latter was too unhandy.

For the rifled flare pistol there was the Wurfkörper 42 LP, a heavy hollow-charge bullet weighing 0.6 kg and able to penetrate 80 mm of armor plate. All these types had an effective range between 30 and 60 meters.

A pistol developed by the Waffen-SS is also worthy of note; it was the Gerloff combat pistol, which was built to fire the 46 and 61 rifle grenades.

Rifle-grenade devices were used by the infantry to attack targets beyond the range of hand grenades. There were two models, the type used by the Army and that with a folding sight, developed by the Luftwaffe for use by the paratroops. Both were used along with the 98k carbine.

The Luftwaffe rifle-grenade device could fire a flight-stabilized rifle grenade developed for antitank use by the WASAG firm. The hollow charge weighed 0.52 kg and could penetrate 45 mm of armor plate.

The antitank projectiles and rifle grenades described here were of great importance to close antitank combat in 1942-43. In the end, their accuracy, range and penetrating power were too meager to be able to keep up with the developments in tank construction. According to evaluations by the troops, their production could be halted in favor of the Panzerfaust, which is what took place in 1944.

For the Army's rifle-grenade device, which fired rifling-stabilized ammunition, the Gewehrpanzergranate (Antitank Rifle Grenade) 30 had already been developed in 1941, but its insufficient penetrating power ruled out its large-scale use. The large antitank rifle grenade became the standard model. The hollow-charge bullet weighed 0.39 kg and could penetrate 80 mm of armor plate. 23,889,000 of them were produced during the war. The SS Weapons Academy brought out two further developments, the Gewehrpanzergranate 46 (90 mm penetration) and the Gewehrpanzergranate 61 (125 mm penetration). For all of these projectiles, the practical range was less than 80 meters. All attempts to increase this resulted in loss of accuracy, and the same was true of an antitank rifle grenade with rocket propulsion. This was also true of the so-called double-shot grenade for the cup discharger, with which experiments were made in 1944.

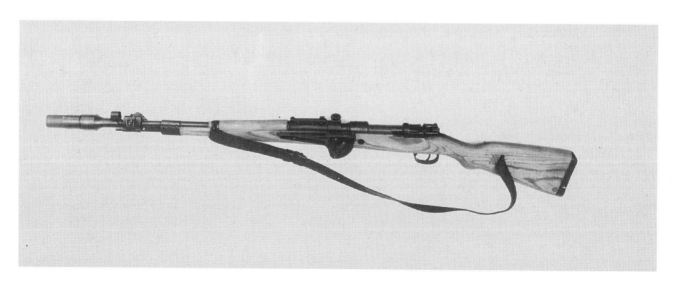

The Carbine 98 k with cup discharger and grenade sight. The cup discharger consists of the rifled barrel that held the grenade.

In the rifle-grenade device –
shown here about to fire explosive
grenades – the infantry possessed
a versatile weapon. If no more
effective weapons and materials
were available, the rifle with its
cup discharger could be used
against light and medium tanks.
During training, according to drill
procedures, quick aiming at
moving tanks was practiced.

Lower left: The antitank rifle
grenade could penetrate only 50
mm of armor plate, which did not
equal requirements. In addition,
the section that fit into the rifling
was made out of aluminum.

Lower center: The
Gewehrpanzergranate 61 attained
high marks with its 125 mm
penetrating power. Because the
Panzerfaust and the
Raketenpanzerbüchse 54 were
already being used by the troops,
it did not achieve any great
significance.

Lower right: The antitank fog
grenade was used to blanket
targets in smoke.

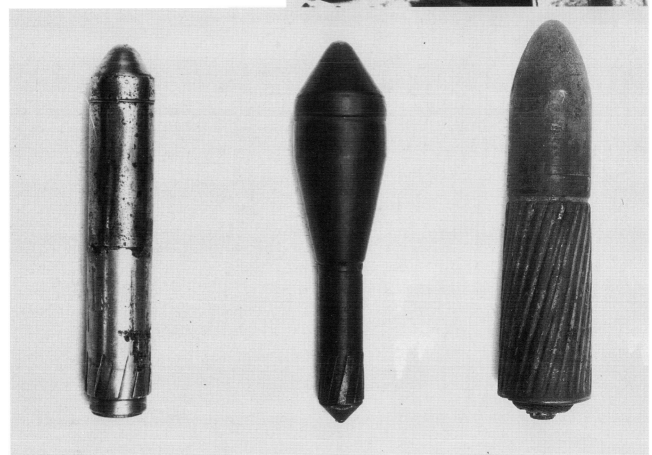

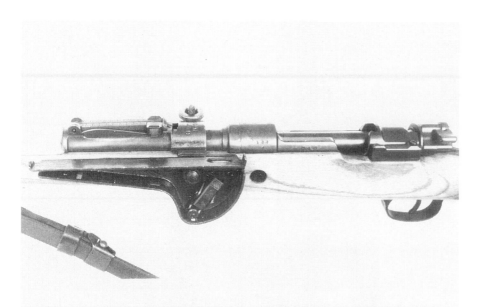

Left:
The grenade sight for the rifle-grenade device was screwed onto the rifle behind the base of the sight, with the help of a retainer.

Below:
The cup discharger was clamped onto the rifle barrel behind the sight carrier with the help of a retainer. At first the rifleman had to insert the rifle grenade into the rifled barrel, and then load the propelling cartridge.

It was used most often: the large Gewehrpanzergranate (80 mm penetrating power). At the right is the hollow bullet of this grenade, and beside it the thorn (80 mm long) which resulted when the bullet penetrated the armor plate.

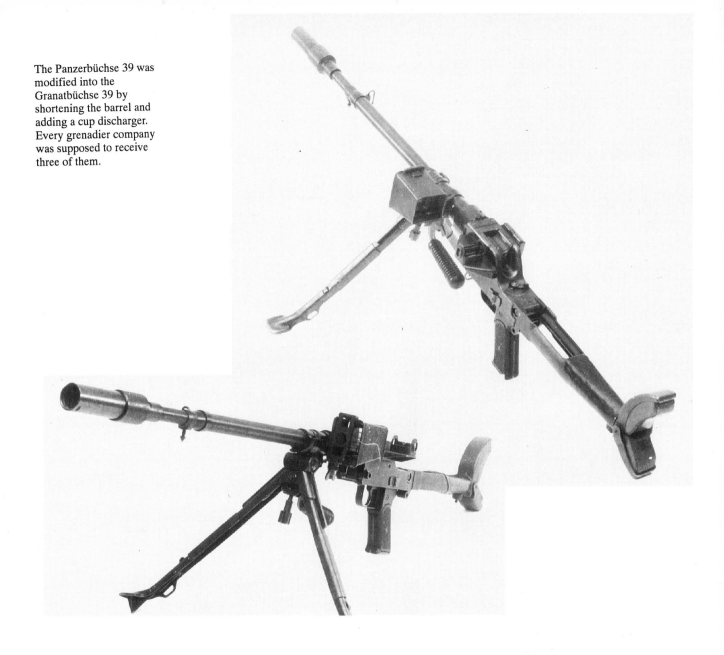

The Panzerbüchse 39 was modified into the Granatbüchse 39 by shortening the barrel and adding a cup discharger. Every grenadier company was supposed to receive three of them.

HAND GRENADES AND ANTITANK MINES

Unlike the Red Army, the Wehrmacht had no special hand grenade for antitank use in 1941. It had, in fact, been advocated in theoretical discussions in the twenties and thirties, but there it had stayed.

Now hectic efforts were being made to make up for the obvious lack of close antitank combat materials by developing antitank hand grenades. The lack of coordination of the developmental work by the Army, Luftwaffe and Waffen-SS also became obvious.

The two-kilogram Panzerhandgranate (Antitank Hand Grenade) 41 could penetrate only 35 mm of armor plate. Test models were presented by the firms of WASAG and Rinker. They were hollow-charge hand grenades. Just as with the developments of the HASAG firm of Leipzig, difficulties arose in stabilizing the flight of the hand grenades sufficiently to make them strike with the point so the impact fuse functioned. This was an absolute prerequisite for the functioning of the hollow charge. There were also difficulties in attaining a significant penetration and keeping the weight low in the interests of a long range at the same time. At HASAG it was realized that the muscle power of the soldier was no longer adequate for an effective antitank weapon.

The antitank mine was developed under contract from the Luftwaffe. It was officially introduced to the paratroops and the Luftwaffe field divisions in May of 1943. This hollow-charge hand grenade had four control surfaces of canvas for stabilization. An improved model, the Panzerwurfmine (kurz), was stabilized by an unrolling strip of cloth and could penetrate 150 mm of armor plate. Neither model proved itself very well, and there were serious accidents in training.

The SS Weapons Academy in Brno proceeded to develop a hollow-charge grenade that had to be stuck onto the wall of the tank. Here the development suggests a hollow charge. The SS also experimented with hollow-charge hand grenades made of Nipolit.

Experiments were also made with incendiary hand grenades. These were glass containers with a mixture of gasoline and benzol or gasoline and heating oil. They were comparable to the incendiary bottles that were made by the troops themselves.

The fog projectiles introduced in 1943 must also be mentioned here. The Blendkörper BK 1 H was soon replaced by the BK 2 H, which was produced and used in great numbers and well known to the troops. It consisted of a glass cover which shattered when it struck the armor, and its contents caused not only smoke but also irritation. Thus the tank crew was often handicapped for some time.

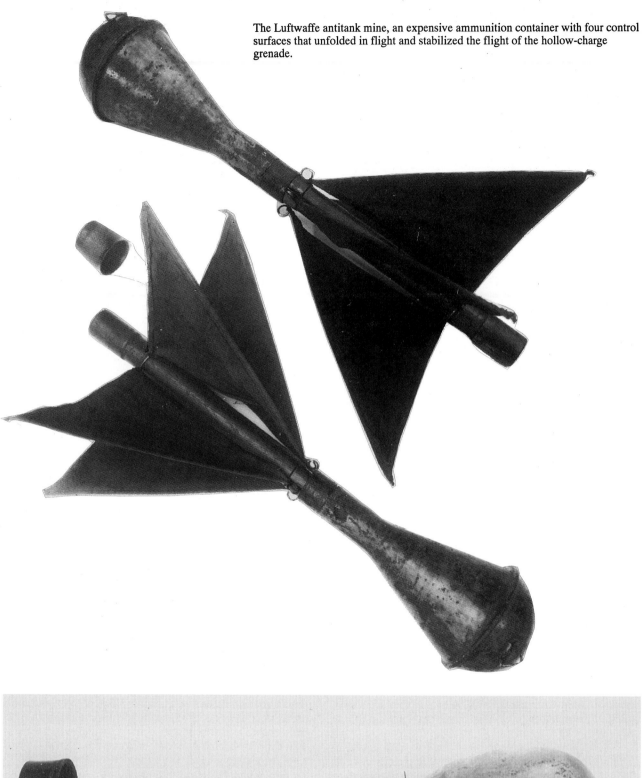

The Luftwaffe antitank mine, an expensive ammunition container with four control surfaces that unfolded in flight and stabilized the flight of the hollow-charge grenade.

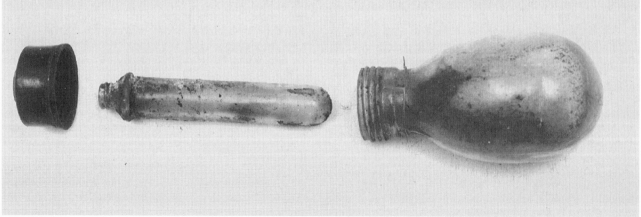

The fog grenade consisted of a pear-shaped glass container and was filled with two different chemicals, which united after the grenade struck and developed a strong and biting fog in the air. Thus the sight of the tank crews was supposed to be obscured.

Left and below:
Through the openings of the tank, especially when the motor was running, it was possible to get enough fog into the fighting compartment . . .

. . . that its effect would cause the crew to disembark. The fog grenade thus created favorable conditions for destroying the tank by makeshift means.

Below:
Fog grenades were stored and transported in boxes of four.

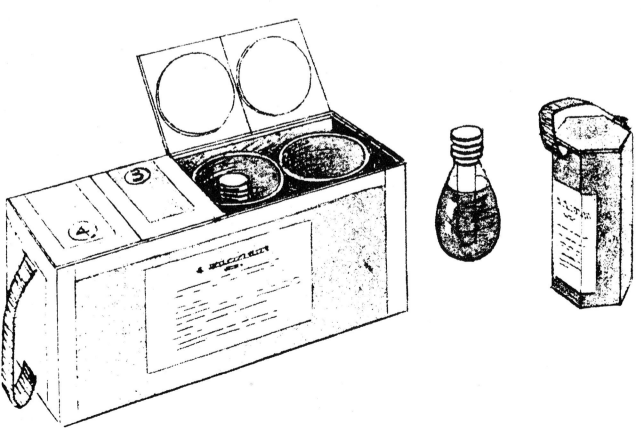

25

ANTITANK HAND MINES AND ATTACHED HOLLOW CHARGES

In May of 1942, a new form of ammunition for close anti-tank combat was tested by the troops on the Volkov – the Panzerhandmine 3. It weighed one kilogram and could penetrate 130 mm of armor plate. Three U-shaped magnets held the mine on the wall of the tank. It and the improved Panzerhandmine 4 had one disadvantage, which they shared with the Hafthohlladung 3 introduced a short time later: The antitank fighter had to get close enough to touch the tank. But direct attachment guaranteed dependable functioning of the hollow charge.

The Hafthohlladung 3 was officially introduced on November 12, 1942, according to information from the OKH. It weighed three kilograms, and its three magnets attached it to the armor plate with a strength of 45 kg. Thus it was possible to destroy even moving tanks under favorable conditions. That and its penetrating power of 140 mm made the attached hollow charge an effective antitank weapon. In 1942, 8500 were made, in 1943 358,400 and in 1944 187,000. In the final version, the Hafthohlladung 3.5, the head of the Panzerfaust was used. With the Panzerfaust, a more effective antitank weapon was provided. For that reason, as stated in an OKH memo of May 15, 1944, the Hafthohlladung could be eliminated completely

Left:
Hafthohlladung 3 (140 mm penetration), and the improved Hafthohlladung 3.5 (160-180 mm penetration). In the latter, the head of the Panzerfaust was used, while both utilized a burning fuse that exploded after 7.5 seconds.

Thus was the Hafthohlladung prepared for use:
1. The fuse with the explosive cap on it was pushed into the neck of the bottle.
2. The iron ring was removed from the magnets.
3. The tear-off cap was unscrewed from the fuse.
Now the Hafthohlladung could be placed on the tank with two poles upward.

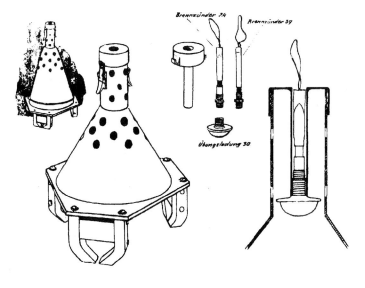

Above:
Training materials for close-combat antitank fighters had to be made by the troops themselves to a great extent. For a practice magnetic hollow charge they needed a wooden funnel, a hand-grenade stick, a set of magnets, a Brennzünder 24 or 39 fuse, an Übungsladung 30 charge, the trigger wire of a Stielhandgranate 24 and the cap of a 7.5 second fuse.

Upper right:
The antitank fighter crouches in a hollow and waits for a tank, in order to attach the hollow charge to it. When the charge was attached to the armor, he had 7.5 seconds after pulling the trigger to seek cover.

Right:
Picture from the summer of 1943, somewhere on the eastern front. An antitank troop, cleverly utilizing the terrain, approaches a tank that has broken through.

FAUSTPATRONE AND PANZERFAUST

In the spring of 1942 the Army Weapons Office again sent out a request to the industries for the development of simple means of antitank combat. The HASAG firm of Leipzig then worked on various, sometimes curious-looking, bodies of ammunition whose effect was based on the hollow-charge principle. Experience that was gained was utilized in the development of a hollow-charge hand grenade, such as had been called for by the Army Weapons Office's WaPrw. 5 of October 3, 1942.

The prescribed throwing range of 40 meters limited the weight to half a kilogram. The light weight in turn limited the penetrating power. For that reason, the HASAG made a suggestion in November of 1942: A hollow charge should be fired from the hand by means of a special cartridge. Tests showed that it was possible to make use of this suggestion.

The development was given the name of Paustpatrone (Fist Cartridge). The caliber of the bullet was 80 mm, the maximum range was 70 meters, and 140 mm of armor plate could be penetrated. The most important innovations of further developments were the replacement of rifling stabilization by wings of spring steel, the lengthening of the cartridge to a barrel 800 mm long, the enlargement of the propellant charge and full recoillessness when firing. The weight of the hollow-charge warhead was raised to 1.3 kilograms. This model went into series production as the Panzerfaust klein. The first 5000 were delivered in August of 1943. Problems in handling became evident at once; the unusually shaped head often slid off the slanted armor of the T-34 tank.

In November of 1942 the Army Weapons Office had called on HASAG for a higher penetrating performance for what was still being developed then as the Faustpatrone. Parallel to the Panzerfaust klein, the Panzerfaust gross (later Panzerfaust 30 m) thus came into being. The warhead weighed 2.9 kilograms now, the charge of black powder was increased from 56 to 95 grams. The optimal range was 30 meters, the maximum 75 meters, and 200 mm of armor plate could be penetrated.

In 1943, 350,000 of the Panzerfaust were produced. Production of the Panzerfaust klein was halted. The HASAG made suggestions to improve the performance and utility of the new weapon. Warheads with shrapnel and incendiary effects were tested. Wa Prw. 11 examined salvo firing devices with ten or sixteen Panzerfaust units.

Despite the deficiencies that were still present, the Panzerfaust established itself as the main close-combat antitank weapon. Production of the Panzerfaust 60 m began in August. The stipulated monthly production of 400,000 units could be attained only in October 1944. Handling had been simplified further and reliability improved. An increase of the black-powder charge to 140 grams necessitated a thicker firing barrel, but brought an increase in the effective range to 75 meters. In November of 1944 the Panzerfaust 100 m came out. The introduction of the hollow-charge cartridge allowed an increase of the effective range to 100 meters while using the old firing barrel. With its trajectory at its greatest height of 3.5 meters, a maximum range of 280 meters could be attained. In December 1944, production reached the striking figure of 1,295,000 units. The misfiring quota, though, was 5.5%!

In the late autumn of 1944, the Army Weapons Office/ Wa Prw. 11 called for a further increase in performance. The range in particular had to be increased. At the same time, the explosive consumption per head (Panzerfaust 100 m: 0.8 kg) was supposed to be decreased without affecting the penetration performance. The uniformity of the warhead of the Panzerfaust with that of the Raketenpanzerbüchse was to be attempted. This development was concluded by HASAG in the spring of 1945, with the result designated Panzerfaust 150 m. An initial contract for 100,000 units was issued, and a few of them were tested by the troops. Their identifying mark was the good aerodynamic design of the warhead.

In the spring of 1945, Panzerfaust production was already being affected by the decline of the German war economy. The Allies systematically destroyed black-powder

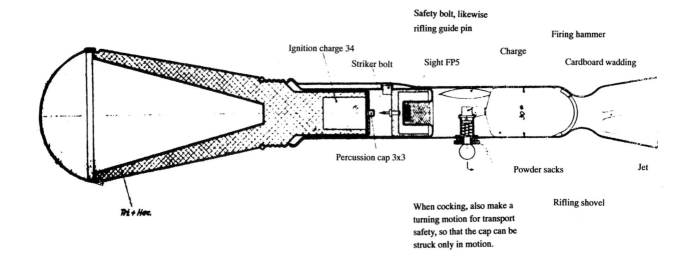

Safety bolt, likewise rifling guide pin

Firing hammer

Ignition charge 34

Charge

Striker bolt

Sight FP5

Cardboard wadding

Percussion cap 3x3

Powder sacks

Jet

Tri + Hex.

When cocking, also make a turning motion for transport safety, so that the cap can be struck only in motion.

Rifling shovel

			Werkstoff					
			Fertiggew.				Änderung	Tag Name
			Maßstab	1:1	Tag	Name	Zeichnung-Nr.	FP 8001
							Ers. durch	
Patent Abgabe							Ersatz für	
·	·				HASAG Leipzig FEA		Faustpatrone 43	

mills in air raids. The need for black powder for the Panzerfaust could not be met, and experiments with nitrocellulose powder were made – not very successfully. Other efforts concentrated on the use of aluminum firing barrels. The reason was that the seamless firing barrels of the Panzerfaust were produced by the iron industry in the Ruhr area, which was already a combat zone.

The Splitterfaust development and the use of splinter rings for the Panzerfaust 150 m must still be mentioned. The further development, the Panzerfaust 250 m, (its range increased by a multi-chambered cartridge that could be reloaded) was not completed in Germany. Test models were finished in the USA after the war under the direction of development teams from HASAG. The development of the Panzerfaust was also evaluated thoroughly in the Soviet Union. The result was the Panzerbüchse RPG-2.

Right: the magnetic hollow charge and Panzerfaust were delivered first to the troops specially trained for close antitank combat. The rest were divided among the company units. Wooden cases and tent canvases were to be used for storage. Damp storage resulted in misfiring.

Below: The Panzerfaust klein weighed 2.7 kg and had an initial velocity of 27 meters per second for the warhead. Its combat range was 30 meters. A large number of the Panzerfaust klein were used by the Romanian Army in 1944.

Right:
The target is sighted, the shooter releases the trigger. Note the awkward handling, seen in the position of the hands, a fault that was eliminated only in the Panzerfaust 60 m.

Below: a close-combat antitank troop ready to go into action. The soldiers are all carrying the Panzerfaust gross (production of which ended in August 1944); the picture was taken on the eastern front in February 1945.

The Panzerfaust played an increasingly important role in propaganda. The headline on the cover of the BERLINER ILLUSTRIERTE ZEITUNG on June 29, 1944 read: "The Panzerfaust! The grenadier's antitank gun."

Propaganda on the other side was also dedicated to this subject. In No. 7 of the periodical FREIES DEUTSCHLAND (published by the National "Free Germany" Committee) of February 11, 1945, there appeared a report: "The Panzerfaust Weapon of Embarrassment."

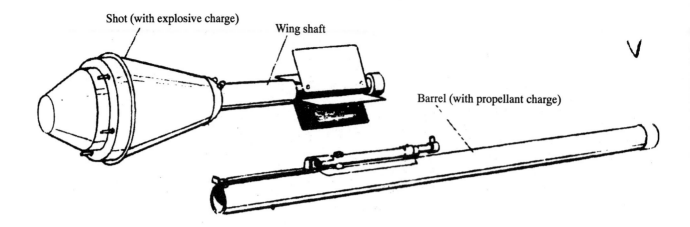

Shot (with explosive charge) Wing shaft

Barrel (with propellant charge)

V

Above: Head and barrel of the Panzerfaust gross. It weighed 5.6 kg, and the initial velocity of the warhead was 27 meters per second. The black-powder charge had been increased from 56 to 95 grams.

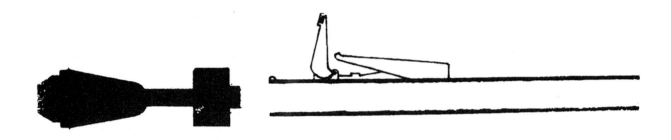

Functioning of the Panzerfaust. No one was allowed to stand within ten meters of the end of the barrel. The head of the Panzerfaust became live about three meters after firing.

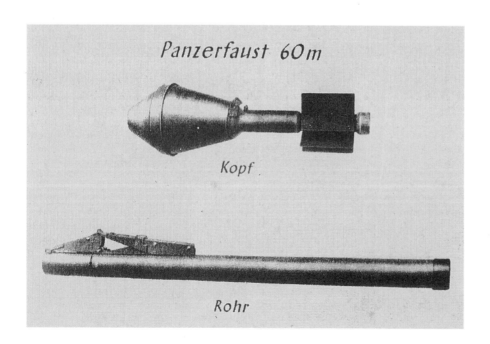

Panzerfaust 60m

Kopf

Rohr

Left:
The head and barrel of the improved Panzerfaust 60 m. Because of the stronger propellant charge (140 grams of black powder), the thickness of the barrel wall was increased by 3 mm. The sight and trigger were improved.

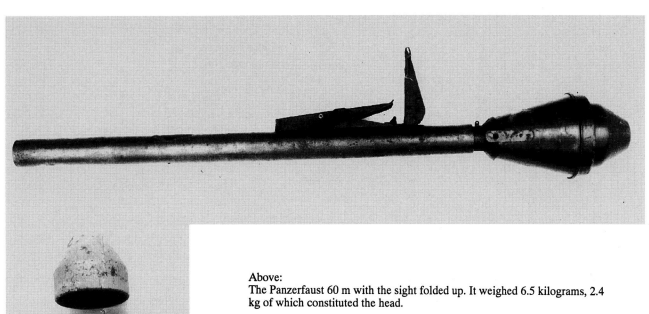

Above:
The Panzerfaust 60 m with the sight folded up. It weighed 6.5 kilograms, 2.4 kg of which constituted the head.

Left:
The dismantled head of a Panzerfaust 60 m. Wooden shaft with wings, funnel with neck (holding the explosive charge of TNT/Hexogen), hollow ball, ballistic head.

Below:
The bow armor plate, weighing more than 550 kilograms, of a Jagdpanzer 38 "Hetzer." It is 60 mm thick and has been pierced twice by Panzerfaust hits – results of a test firing. Displayed in the Museum of Military History, Dresden.

Zündladungen und Zünder

The Panzerfaust was delivered in wooden cases holding four units.

Right:
Priming the Panzerfaust 60 m: The head was pulled out of the barrel, the wing shaft remained in the barrel. Then (head down) the Zündladung 34 and the fuse were inserted.

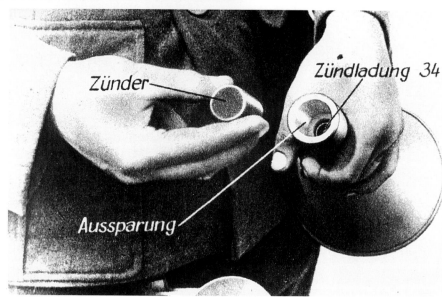

Zünder — *Zündladung 34*

Aussparung

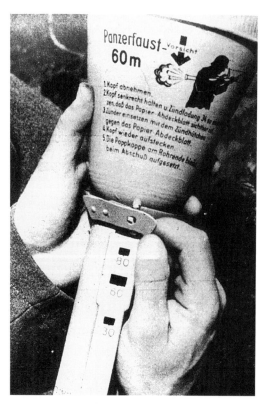

Important directions for using the Panzerfaust were stamped on the head and barrel. Printed directions were also included.

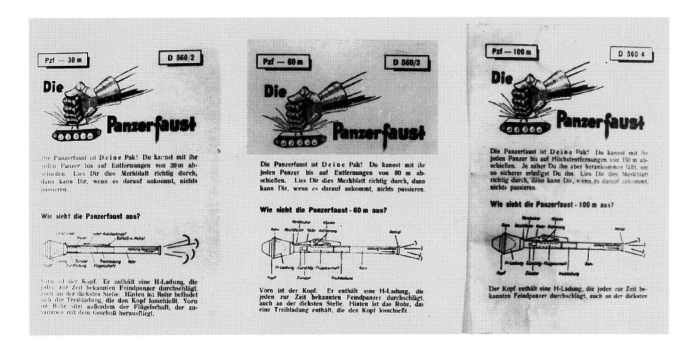

Above:
Printed instructions for the
Panzerfaust 30 m, 60 m and 100 m.

Right:
The simple operation of the
Panzerfaust was supposed to allow
its use after only brief training. This
was of great importance for its use,
especially by the Volkssturm. For the
weekly newsreels, women demon-
strated how simple it was to use the
"wonder weapon" Panzerfaust.

The Panzerfaust 100 m with its sight folded up. With it, the combat range of the Panzerfaust could be increased to 100 meters. The bulky
head was not satisfactory, and the high consumption of explosive was criticized.

There were various ways of firing the Panzerfaust:
Above: Overarm firing, used especially when firing from holes and ditches. Below: Armpit firing, customary when firing from under cover.

Right: The Panzerfaust 60 m provided significant improvements. With a range of 60 meters, 75-80% hits were scored; at 80 meters, the percentage sank to 25%.

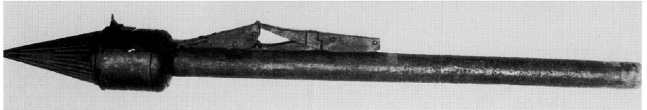

The Panzerfaust 150 m had the hollow-charge cartridge of the previous model (2x95 grams of black powder as a propellant charge). The aerodynamically well-formed head attained a maximum velocity of 85 meters per second. The resemblance to the Russian RPG-2 antitank weapon of postwar days is striking and not accidental.

The head of one of the many test models in the Panzerfaust series. Only a few examples are still in existence, some of them fragmentary. They document the numerous experiments made by HASAG of Leipzig with the goal of increasing the performance of the Panzerfaust.

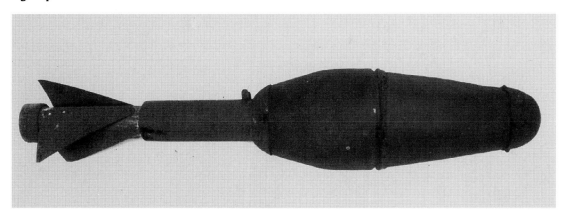

Above: Members of a tank destroyer unit with Panzerfaust and Raketenpanzerbüchse.

Below: Frankfurt an der Oder, spring 1945. Members of an antitank command, formed primarily of Hitler Youth members, ride through the streets and into action. Once in a while these bicycle units were able to achieve success, but in general, the dilemma of German antitank defense in 1945 became obvious in these and other attempts.

RAKETENLANZERBÜCHSE
(OFENROHR, PANZERSCHRECK)

In Illustrated Brochure 149a "Panzernahkampfwaffen Part 1 Panzerschreck" (Addendum to H.Dv. 469/4) of November 14, 1944, the 8.8 cm Raketenpanzerbüchse 54 is characterized as a recoilless hand weapon for use against all tanks at ranges up to 150 meters. Its development was assisted by the American "Bazooka" antitank weapon which had been captured in Tunisia and brought to Kummersdorf for testing. The demand for greater penetrating power resulted in the caliber being enlarged to 88 mm (the "Bazooka" was 60 mm). A considerable improvement was electric ignition by means of a shock generator.

The Raketenpanzerbüchse weighed 9.25 kilograms empty and was 1640 mm long. Low weight and very simple handling made it suitable for front-line antitank use. The first models had no protective shield. The shooter had to make do with gauntlets, a head covering or a gas mask without a filter to protect himself from the bits of powder that flew backward. As of October 1943, the improved Raketenpanzerbüchse 54 was produced. It had a protective shield with a sighting window and weighed 11 kilograms. According to instructions from the OKH, the official introduction of this antitank weapon took place only effective August 20, 1944. But an initial contract for 382,000 of the Raketenpanzerbüchse had already been filled in July 1944.

At first it fired the Raketenpanzerbüchsen-Granate 4322. This weighed 3.25 kilograms, was stabilized by a ring-shaped control surface, and could penetrate 160 mm of armor. It was made as summer ammunition (to fire at -5 to +50 degrees) and as winter ammunition (to fire at -40 to +30 degrees). The ammunition was improved steadily – the 4992 version achieved an effective range of 180 meters – but also developed serious problems. Up to 12.9% were rejected on delivery.

Early in 1945 the improved Raketenpanzerbüchse 54/1 went into production. The contract called for 48,000 units. They had a shorter barrel and improved aiming. As of December 1944, the Raketenpanzerbüchse 54 was modified into the new model. The life span of the barrel was 200 rounds.

Further developments of the Raketenpanzerbüchse went in various directions. In August of 1943 a larger model of 10.5 cm caliber had been suggested. Uniformity of the warhead with the Panzerfaust 150 m was attempted. The SS Weapons Academy had test models of impregnated pressed cardboard made.

For use by the Panzerjäger units of the Panzergrenadier battalions (SPW), precise directions for the installation of racks for mounting the Raketenpanzerbüchse on the armored personnel carrier (Sd.Kfz. 251) were published in the Army Technical Instruction Brochures of January 15, 1945.

Despite the good results attained with the Raketenpanzerbüchse, the cessation of its production was foreseen. In the Army's assault program, an armament study of January 9, 1945, one can read under the heading of close antitank combat materials: "A close antitank combat device is to be striven for, whereby the Panzerfaust will be given priority according to previous experience. In the limitation to one type, the need for the Panzerfaust would increase from 600,000 to 800,000 (per month)."

Right:
Am American "Bazooka" captured in North Africa. It was the starting point for the development of the "Panzerschreck" (later renamed "Raketenpanzerbüchse").

The early form of the Raketenpanzerbüchse. A protective shield with a sighting window was added only later. The equipment of a mountain Jäger division in 1944 was supposed to include 117 of them.

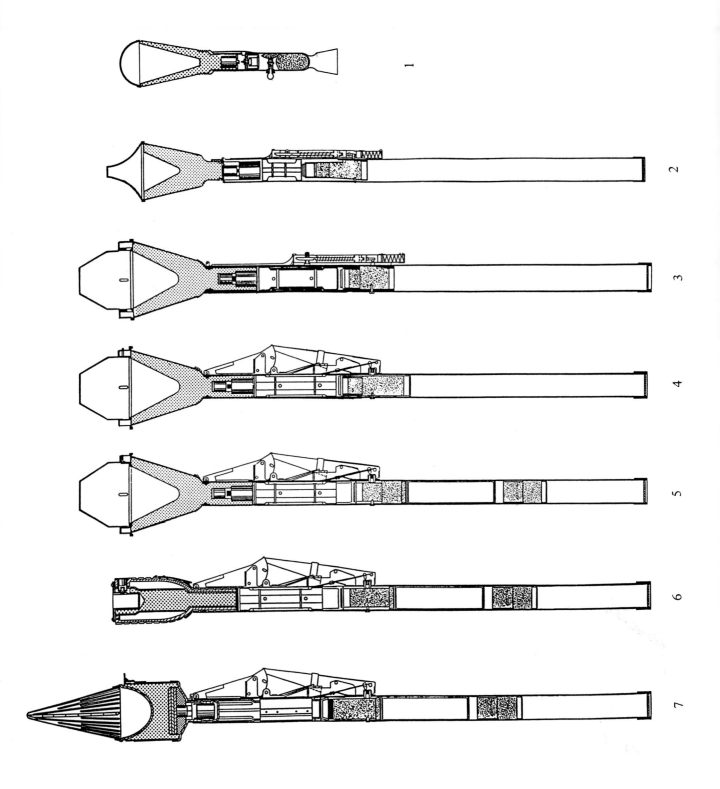

1. Faustpatrone,

2. Panzerfaust klein (also called
Faustpatrone 1 until May 1944),

3. Panzerfaust gross (also called
Faustpatrone 2 until May 1944),

4. Panzerfaust 60 m,

5. Panzerfaust 100 m,

6. Splitterfaust,

7. Panzerfaust 150 m.

Right::
The lack of a protective shield on the Raketenpanzerbüchse resulted in shooters being burned by powder particles flying backward. Motorcycle jacket, gloves and a mask provided protection until the weapon was equipped with a shield.

Below:
In order to rule out temperature differences as a cause of deficiencies in accuracy, the sight was equipped with appropriate markings. Moving tanks were fired on from distances up to 120 meters.

Lower right:
The trigger system with safety and shock generator.

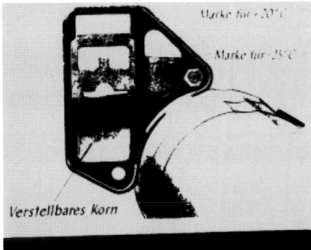

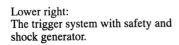

Verstellbares Korn

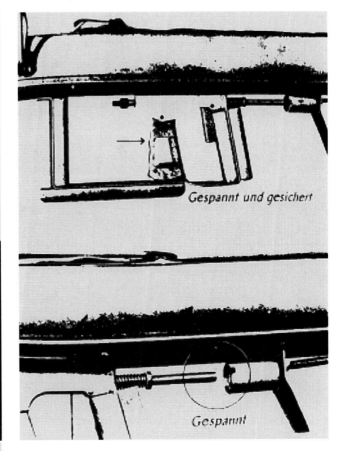

Gespannt und gesichert

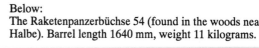

Gespannt

Below:
The Raketenpanzerbüchse 54 (found in the woods near Halbe). Barrel length 1640 mm, weight 11 kilograms.

Various firing positions were also used for the Raketenpanzerbüchse 54. The safest manner was the lying position. The gunner and loader had to lie at a right angle to the weapon. The kneeling and standing positions were used only from cover.

Second only to the meager effective range of the Raketenpanzerbüchse, its lack of mobility in comparison to the tank was its worst disadvantage for the tank-destroyer battalion. Almost all of these units were horse-drawn. In each of the three groups of the tank-destroyer platoons of a company, two If.8 infantry carts were available, which could be drawn in tandem by one horse and could transport six of the Raketenpanzerbüchse with thirty rounds of ammunition.

An If.8 infantry cart as used to transport six of the Raketenpanzerbüchse and, along with a second wagon, the thirty rounds of ammunition for a tank-destroyer group.

A tank-destroyer troop waited for the attacking tank is safe cover. Little time remained for an effective attack on the target once the tank had driven into the effective range. The tank could cover 150 meters in less than a minute.

Back carriers were made of wood by the troops themselves to carry five Raketenpanzerbüchse grenades.

Left:
The loader with a back carrier holding five Raketenpanzerbüchse grenades. One shell weighed 3.25 kilograms; its initial velocity was about 110 meters per second.

The Raketenpanzerbüchse 54/1 was shorter (1350 mm) than the earlier model, and weighed 9.5 kilograms. Five rounds per minute could be fired. The cost of a weapon was some 70 Reichsmark, and ten work hours were needed to produce it. It was manufactured by: HASAG of Meuselwitz, Enzinger Union-Werke of Pfeddersheim near Worms, Schricker & Co. of Vach near Nürnberg, Kronprinz of Schlingen-Ohligs, Jäckel of Freistadt in Upper Silesia, and Scheffler Brothers of Berlin.

Above:
In firing position. In a report on the waging of war in Posen of March 1, 1945, the effectiveness of the Raketenpanzerbüchse was particularly emphasized. In addition to tanks, positions with antitank guns and infantry targets at ranges of up to 1000 meters were attacked.

Left:
In the collection of the Military History Museum in Dresden are these two test models. The rocket launchers came from the Kummersdorf firing range. No further information is available.

PERFORMANCE CHART FOR ARMOR-PIERCING WEAPONS AND CLOSE-COMBAT DEVICES

Weapon	Ammunition	Penetration	Effective Range
Rifle	Pointed bullet with core	8 mm	100 meters
	Antitank rifle grenade 30	50 mm	40 meters
	Large antitank rifle grenade	80 mm	80 meters
	Antitank rifle grenade 46	90 mm	60-80 meters
	Antitank rifle grenade 61	125 mm	60-80 meters
	Antitank rifle grenade GGP	45 mm	
Smooth-bore flare pistol	Wurfkörper 326 HL/LP	50 mm	
Rifled flare pistol	Panzerwurfkörper 42 LP	80 mm	75 meters
Panzerbüchse 38	Pointed bullet with core H Rs L'Spur	25 mm	300 meters
Panzerbüchse 39	"	"	"
Granatbüchse 39	Large antitank rifle grenade	80 mm	80 meters
Panzerbüchse 35 (P)	Pointed bullet with core H Rs	30 mm	100 m
Panzerbüchse 783 (r)	Pointed bullet with core Br	30 mm	100 meters
Panzerbüchse 784 (r)	"	"	"
	Antitank hand grenade 41	30 mm	10-15 meters
	Antitank throwing mine (short)	150 mm	25 meters
	Antitank hand mine 3	130 mm	0 meters
	Antitank hand mine 4	150 mm	0 meters
	Hollow charge 3	140 mm	0 meters
	Hollow charge 3.5	180 mm	0 meters
	T-mine 35	80-100 mm	0 meters
	Clustered charge 3 Kg	60 mm	0 mm
	Faustpatrone	140 mm	70 meters (maximum)
	Panzerfaust klein	140 mm	30 meters
	Panzerfaust gross (30 m)	200 mm	30 meters
	Panzerfaust 60 m	200 mm	60-75 meters
	Panzerfaust 100 m	200 mm	100 meters
	Panzerfaust 150 m	220 mm	150 meters
	Panzerfaust 250 m	220 mm	250-300 meters
Raketenpanzerbüchse 54 **Raketenpanzerbüchse 54/1**	Raketenpanzerbüchse grenade	160 mm	150-180 meters
Raketenpanzerbüchse 10.5 cm	Raketenpanzerbüchse grenade	220 mm	

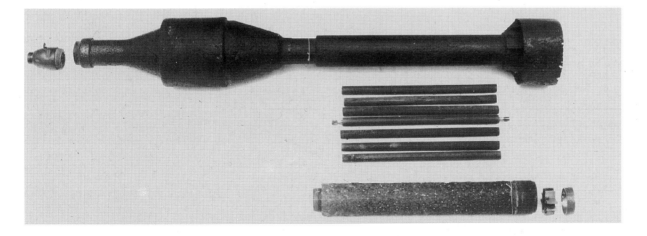

A Raketenpanzerbüchse Grenade 4322. The main components are the warhead with impact fuse, the combustion chamber with jet and control surfaces. In the combustion chamber are seven rods of powder, one of them with ignition.

Also from the publisher

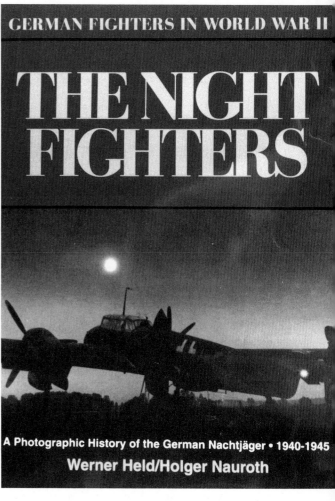